FAVORITE TOYS

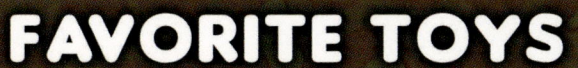

SKATEBOARDS

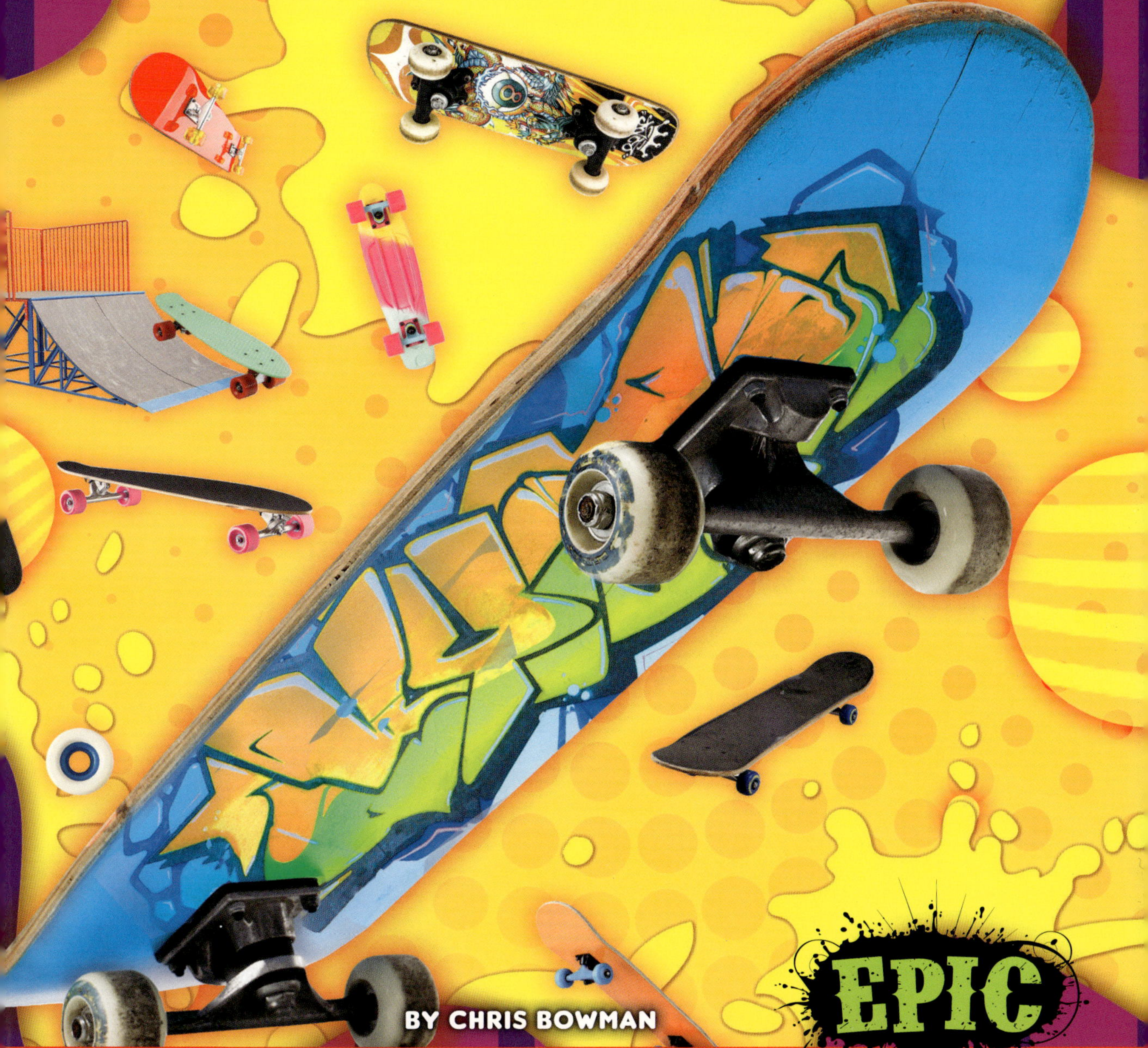

BY CHRIS BOWMAN

EPIC

BELLWETHER MEDIA · MINNEAPOLIS, MN

Action and adventure collide in EPIC. Plunge into a universe of powerful beasts, hair-raising tales, and high-speed excitement. Astonishing explorations await. Can you handle it?

This edition first published in 2022 by Bellwether Media, Inc.

No part of this publication may be reproduced in whole or in part without written permission of the publisher. For information regarding permission, write to Bellwether Media, Inc., Attention: Permissions Department, 6012 Blue Circle Drive, Minnetonka, MN 55343.

Library of Congress Cataloging-in-Publication Data
Names: Bowman, Chris, 1990- author.
Title: Skateboards / by Chris Bowman.
Description: Minneapolis, MN : Bellwether Media, Inc., 2022. | Series: Epic : Favorite toys | Includes bibliographical references and index. | Audience: Ages 7-12 | Audience: Grades 2-3 | Summary: "Engaging images accompany information about skateboards. The combination of high-interest subject matter and light text is intended for students in grades 2 through 7"–Provided by publisher.
Identifiers: LCCN 2021044248 (print) | LCCN 2021044249 (ebook) | ISBN 9781644876381 (library binding) | ISBN 9781648346491 (ebook)
Subjects: LCSH: Skateboards–Juvenile literature.
Classification: LCC GV859.8 .B692 2022 (print) | LCC GV859.8 (ebook) | DDC 796.22–dc23
LC record available at https://lccn.loc.gov/2021044248
LC ebook record available at https://lccn.loc.gov/2021044249

Text copyright © 2022 by Bellwether Media, Inc. EPIC and associated logos are trademarks and/or registered trademarks of Bellwether Media, Inc.

Editor: Elizabeth Neuenfeldt   Designer: Josh Brink

Printed in the United States of America, North Mankato, MN.

TABLE OF CONTENTS

Getting Air! 4
The History of Skateboards .. 6
Skateboards Today 14
More Than A Toy 20
Glossary 22
To Learn More 23
Index 24

Getting Air!

A skater wants to try a trick. It is called an **ollie**. She stomps on the back of the board. Then her foot catches the front of the board. She lands it! Skateboards let people do fun tricks.

The History of Skateboards

Skateboards were **invented** in the early 1900s. At first, skateboards were homemade. Some people put roller skate wheels on boards. Others removed handles from scooters.

STORE-BOUGHT SKATEBOARDS IN 1964

SKATEBOARD BEGINNINGS

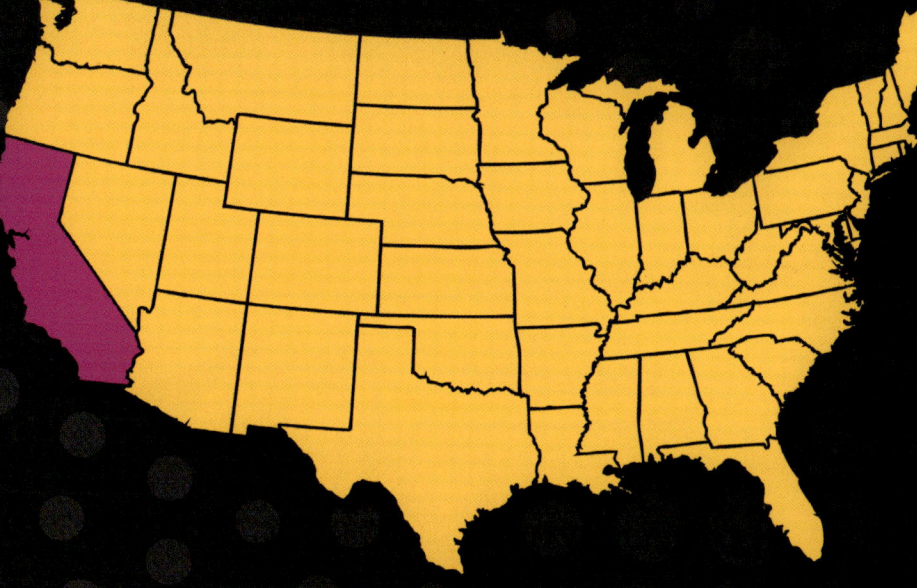

California, United States = 🟣

Skateboards were first sold in stores in California in 1959.

Skateboarding quickly became popular. More than 50 million boards were sold by the mid-1960s!

1960s SKATEBOARDS

MAKING WAVES

Surfers helped make skateboards popular. Skateboarding was first known as "sidewalk surfing."

But early skateboards were unsafe. Skateboarders kept getting hurt. People soon lost interest in skateboarding.

Skateboards became safer in the 1970s. New wheels were added to skateboards in 1972. They gripped the ground better.

REINVENTING THE WHEEL

EARLY SKATEBOARDS WERE MADE WITH CLAY WHEELS. WHEELS ARE NOW MADE OF A KIND OF PLASTIC AND RUBBER.

Kicktails were also added to skateboard **decks**. They helped skateboarders stay balanced.

Skateboarding grew during the 1980s. Skaters built their own ramps.
They also began to do tricks around cities. This is known as **street skateboarding**. This **style** remains popular today!

STREET SKATEBOARDING

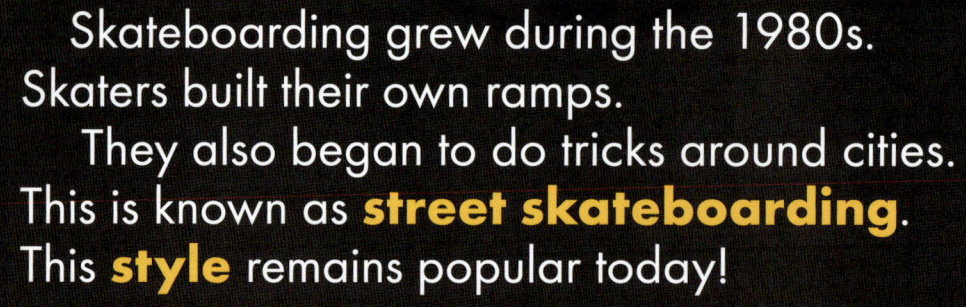

SCREEN TIME

VIDEOS OF SKATERS HAVE HELPED THE SPORT GROW. FANS CAN WATCH THEIR FAVORITE SKATERS DO NEW TRICKS!

SKATEBOARD TIMELINE

1963
The first skateboard competition is held in Hermosa Beach, California

1959
The first skateboards are sold by Roller Derby in California

1972
New types of wheels are added to skateboards

1995
The first X Games is held in Rhode Island

Skateboards Today

There are many kinds of skateboard decks. Standard skateboards have hard wheels. They are often used for tricks.

CRUISER

Cruisers are short and easy to carry. They work well for getting around.

15

Longboards can cover a lot of ground. They have longer decks and offer skaters a relaxing ride.

Old-school skateboards have wider decks. The wheels are placed farther apart. They help skaters ride in **bowls**.

BOWL

SKATEBOARD TYPES

standard

cruiser

old-school

longboard

There are different skating styles, too. **Park skateboarding** is commonly done at **skate parks**.

PARK SKATEBOARDING

VERT SKATEBOARDING

Vert skateboarding is another favorite style. Riders skateboard in large ramps. There is a skateboarding style for every kind of rider!

More Than A Toy

Skateboarding is a popular sport. Fans love watching skaters **compete** in the X Games and the **Olympics**.
Skateboards are fun for people of all ages!

2020 OLYMPICS

20

X GAMES PROFILE

What Is It? A worldwide extreme sports competition

When Did It Start? 1995

Where Does It Happen? Different places around the world

How Often Does It Happen? Twice a year

X GAMES 2017

Glossary

bowls—parts of skate parks with curved walls; bowls are made to look like empty pools.

compete—to try to win something that someone else is also trying to win

decks—the parts of skateboards that riders stand on

invented—made for the first time

kicktails—the raised ends of skateboard decks

ollie—a skateboard trick in which the rider hits the back of the board in order to jump with the board

Olympics—a series of global sports competitions that are held as separate winter and summer events in a different country every four years

park skateboarding—a style of skateboarding in which riders often do tricks on many different objects

skate parks—areas with ramps, rails, and other objects where skateboarders can skate and do tricks

street skateboarding—a style of skateboarding that includes riding on ramps, rails, and other objects that could be found around a city

style—a way of doing something

vert skateboarding—a style of skateboarding that usually takes place on large ramps

To Learn More

AT THE LIBRARY

Chandler, Matt. *Nyjah Huston: Skateboard Superstar.* North Mankato, Minn.: Capstone Press, 2021.

Kenney, Karen Latchana. *Extreme Skateboarding Challenges.* Minneapolis, Minn.: Lerner Publications, 2021.

Sommer, Nathan. *Bicycles.* Minneapolis, Minn.: Bellwether Media, 2022.

ON THE WEB

FACTSURFER

Factsurfer.com gives you a safe, fun way to find more information.

1. Go to www.factsurfer.com.

2. Enter "skateboards" into the search box and click 🔍.

3. Select your book cover to see a list of related content.

Index

beginnings, 7
bowls, 16
California, 7
cruisers, 15
decks, 11, 14, 16
history, 6, 7, 8, 9, 10, 11
kicktails, 11
longboards, 16
Olympics, 20
park skateboarding, 18
profile, 21
ramps, 12, 19
safety, 9, 10

sales, 7, 8
skate parks, 18
street skateboarding, 12
styles, 12, 18, 19
surfers, 9
timeline, 13
tricks, 4, 12, 14
types, 17
vert skateboarding, 19
videos, 12
wheels, 6, 10, 14
X Games, 20, 21

The images in this book are reproduced through the courtesy of: rCarner, front cover (hero), back cover (bottom right); Birgit Reitz-Hofmann, front cover (middle top skateboard), p. 22; Polad Gasimov, front cover (top left); Lilkin, front cover (top right, wheel); HomeArt, front cover (red skateboard, bottom left), back cover (bottom left); Dzha33, front cover (pink cruiser), back cover (top right); Olga Kovalenko, front cover (back deck); al7, front cover (longboard); fotoslaz, back cover (top left), p. 17 (standard); Dmitry Zimin, back cover (middle left); Heike Brauer, back cover (bottom right); CapturePB, p. 2 (wooden skateboard); ganjalex, p. 2 (cruiser); Nor Gal, p. 2; lzf, pp. 4-5; Floyd H. McCall/ Getty Images, p. 6; dpa/ Alamy, p. 8; Bettmann/ Getty Images, p. 9; D. Corson/ ClassicStock/ Getty Images, p. 10; Pavel Ilyukhin, p. 11; FelixRenaud, p. 12; seeshooteatrepeat, p. 13 (standard wheels); Juan Camilo Bernal, pp. 13 (X Games), 21 (logo); frantic00, p. 14; Volodymyr Tverdokhlib/ Alamy, p. 15; Mega Pixel, p. 15 (helmet straps); Venice Beach Photos, p. 16; BonD80, p. 17 (cruiser); Tim Thompson/ Alamy, p. 17 (old school); Dumitrusphotography, p. 17 (longboard); homydesign, p. 18; A. Einsiedler, p. 19; A.RICARDO, p. 20; Tribune Content Agency LLC/ Alamy, p. 21; al7, p. 23.